Sporting Wit

Athletic Wisecracks and Champion Comebacks

summersdale

SPORTING WIT

Summersdale Publishers Ltd
46 West Street
Chichester
West Sussex
PO19 1RP
UK

www.summersdale.com

Disclaimer
Every effort has been made to obtain the necessary
permissions with reference to copyright material, both
illustrative and quoted; should there be any omissions in
this respect we apologise and shall be pleased to make the
appropriate acknowledgements in any future edition.

Printed and bound in Great Britain

ISBN 1 84024 455 0

Editor's note

Sport isn't funny – how could anything be more serious? But as the late, great Peter Ustinov said, comedy is only an amusing way of being serious. And sometimes you've just got to see the funny side – even when that side isn't doing so well.

All the pleasures and the pains of the sporting world are eloquently expressed within the following pages in some of the wittiest words uttered both on and off the pitch. In order to create a complete compendium, we scoured stadiums around the world to bring you the bon mots from every sporting occasion, from the players, the managers, the commentators and the fans. We included a few classics as well as the latest gems, proving that, despite blows to the head and other field injuries, there are plenty of true wits in the sporting world.

Perhaps you'll thumb immediately to the pages on your favourite sport, but don't miss the priceless comments on many others as well as in such categories as Refs and Umpires, Winning and Losing, and The Sporting Life. We hope you'll be as thoroughly entertained as we were, and find these witty words a perfect aid to post-game discussions.

Contents

Sporting Wit

Football

I'd rather be a footballer
than an existentialist.
Robert Smith, British musician

———

The hardest part of football is
putting the ball into the net.
Roy Keane, football player

———

When I first heard about Viagra,
I thought it was a new player
Chelsea had just signed.
Tony Banks, British sports minister

Ally MacLeod thinks that tactics are a new kind of mint.

Billy Connolly, British comedian

When I first met him I didn't know whether to shake his hand or lick his face.

Robbie Williams, British singer, on meeting David Beckham

They are a young side. It's like when you were eighteen with three girlfriends. The more you play, the more you learn.

Mick Walker, British football player

That's great, tell
him he's Pelé and
get him back on.

John Lambie, football manager, on being told that
a concussed striker did not know who he was

Look, if you're in the penalty area and aren't quite sure what to do with the ball, just stick it in the net and we'll discuss all your options afterwards.

Bob Paisley, football manager (1919–1996)

Anyone can be clever, the trick is not to think the other guy is stupid.

Jose Mourinho, football manager

How do I view United? Preferably on television, but unfortunately we have to go down the East Lancs Road and get a bit closer.

Howard Kendall, football manager

White Hart Lane is a great
place. The only thing wrong
is the seats face the pitch.

Les Dawson, British comedian (1934–1993),
referring to the home of Tottenham Hotspur

Preston. They're one of my
old clubs. But then most of
them are. I've had more clubs
than Jack Nicklaus.

Tommy Docherty, football player and manager

Some you lose, some you draw.

Jasper Carrott, comedian, on being
a Birmingham City supporter

The only way we will
be going to Europe
is if the club splash
out and take us all
to EuroDisney.

Dean Holdsworth, football player

British ferries have stopped transporting live animals to the Continent. This has made it very difficult for England fans to get to away matches.

Jo Brand, comedienne

———◆———

We'll still be happy if we lose. It's on at the same time as the Beer Festival.

Noel O'Mahony, football manager, before a game in Munich

———◆———

Radio football is football reduced to its lowest common denominator. Shorn of the game's aesthetic pleasures, or the comfort of a crowd that feels the same way as you, or the sense of security that you get when you see that your defenders and goalkeeper are more or less where they should be, all that is left is naked fear.

Nick Hornby, novelist, *Fever Pitch*

Football is a simple game
made unnecessarily
complicated by managers.

Anonymous

This is an unusual Scotland side
because they have good players.

**Javier Clemente, Spanish coach, on
Scotland's 1996 Under-21 side**

I spent a lot of money on
booze, birds and fast cars.
The rest I just squandered.

George Best, football player

It's a pleasure to be standing
up here. It's a pleasure
to be standing up.

**George Best, acceptance speech on being
acclaimed Footballer of the Century in 1999**

Reporter: You don't take losing lightly, do you Gordon?
Strachan: I don't take stupid comments lightly either.

———•———

Reporter: Gordon, you must be delighted with that result?
Strachan: You're spot on! You can read me like a book.

———•———

On being asked his opinion of Agustin Delgado –
Strachan: I've got more important things to think about. I've got a yoghurt to finish by today, the expiry date is today. That can be my priority rather than Agustin Delgado.

Reporter: This might sound like a daft question, but you'll be happy to get your first win under your belt, won't you?
Strachan: You're right. It is a daft question. I'm not even going to bother answering that one.

Reporter: Bang, there goes your unbeaten run. Can you take it?
Strachan: No, I'm just going to crumble like a wreck. I'll go home, become an alcoholic and maybe jump off a bridge. Umm, I think I can take it, yeah.

Gordon Strachan, football player, voted Scottish Footballer of the Year in 1980 and English Footballer of the Year in 1992, and football manager

Football is like politics: you think
you have won and then you haven't.

**Silvio Berlusconi, AC Milan owner
and prime minister of Italy**

———•———

Thierry has been absolutely
magical and I love the way he plays
the game and expresses himself.
He is like Merlin the Magician
and Dr Who rolled into one.

Gordon Taylor, PFA chief, on Arsenal's Thierry Henry

———•———

*After Sergei Bubka asked for $40,000 to
appear at a Crystal Palace meeting –*

Sergei, I'm only asking you
to compete, I don't want to
buy the Soviet Union.

Andy Norman

Robert Maxwell has just bought Brighton and Hove Albion, and he's furious to find it is only one club.

Tommy Docherty

Some of our players can hardly write their own names, but you should see them add up.

Karl-Heinz Thielen, German football manager, on his squad and their pay packets

The trouble with a lot of our players is that they've got Frank Sinatra tastes and Frank Ifield voices.

Francis Lee, former international footballer who took over as chairman of Manchester City, on the club's overpaid and underachieving squad

As for wages, the players have had a trim, the chairman has had a trim and I have had a short back and sides.

Harry Redknapp, football manager

I hope we get a decision shortly – I will be dead soon.

Stuart Pearce, football player, on wanting to be made Manchester City manager

---

I rung Kenny Jackett straight away to congratulate him on getting Swansea promoted and he said 'I'm waiting to get my goalie out of jail'. You can't even celebrate these days, can you?

Ian Holloway, football manager

I tell you another crazy, crazy, crazy rule. We want women to come to football don't we? You talk to women about footballers and what do they like – they like legs and our shorts are getting longer. We should go back to the days when half your arse was hanging out.

Ian Holloway

Why can't you let players lift up their shirts? Who is it disrespecting? What's wrong with letting a load of young ladies see a good-looking lad take his shirt off? They'd have to watch other teams, though – because my team is as ugly as hell.

Ian Holloway

We're feeling lower than a snake's belly.

Graeme Souness, football manager, after
seeing his side crash out of the UEFA and
FA Cups in the space of four days

The fat lady hasn't started to sing yet, but she has a mic in her hand.

Ian Holloway

It was more fight club than football club – and the usual suspects.

Gary Lineker, football player and commentator

We've been going down quicker than the Titanic.

Chris Turner, football manager, upon relegation

My magic words at half-time
were fuck, bollocks, bastard,
crap and piss-poor.
Mick McCarthy, football manager

Why is there only one ball for 22
players? If you gave a ball to each
of them they'd stop fighting for it.
Unknown

The first ninety minutes
of a football match are
the most important.
Bobby Robson, football manager

Some people think football is a
matter of life and death. I don't like
that attitude. I can assure them it
is much more serious than that.

Bill Shankly, football manager (1914–1981)

———•———

You base football player!

William Shakespeare, *King Lear*

I'll stay in football.
I don't mind if they
stand me up and use
me as a corner flag.

Derek Dooley, football player, after
having his leg amputated

American Football

For when the One Great Scorer comes
    To write against your name,
He marks not that you won or lost
    But how you played the game.
Joe Theismann, American football player

It is, I know, naughty to commit
    sociology promiscuously, but if
you hold up football to the bright
light of the social sciences you will
see that it mirrors modern life. It is
committee meetings, called huddles,
separated by outbursts of violence.
George F. Will, US editor, commentator and columnist

Winning is the science of
    being totally prepared.
George Allen, American football coach (1922–1990)

Sure, luck means a lot in football. Not having a good quarterback is bad luck.

Don Schula, American football coach

He carries so many tacklers with him, he's listed in the Yellow Pages under 'Public Transportation'.

Bob Hope, US comedian and actor (1903–2003), on Marcus Allen, American football player

---

Football is not a contact sport. Football is a collision sport. Dancing is a contact sport.

Duffy Daugherty, American football coach (1915–1987)

Rugby is a beastly game played by gentlemen; soccer is a gentleman's game played by beasts; football is a beastly game played by beasts.

Henry Blaha, rugby player

If women were meant to play football, God would have put their tits somewhere else.

Gordon Sinclair, Canadian journalist and author (1900–1984)

———•———

Pro football is like nuclear warfare. There are no winners, only survivors.

Frank Gifford, American football player

———•———

Football is nothing like life. It's organized and neat and rational. Everyone is either with you or against you and the boundaries are straight lines that are clearly marked. The only sport that's like life is bullfighting, and only for the bull.

King Kaufman, sportswriter, on Rush Limbaugh's comment that 'football is a lot like life'

The football season is like
pain. You forget how terrible
it is until it seizes you again.

Sally Quinn, US journalist

One man practising sportsmanship
is better than a hundred teaching it.

Knute Rockne, American football coach (1888–1931)

Athletics

My first 18-foot pole vault wasn't any more of a thrill than my first clearance at 15 or 16 or 17 foot. I just had more time to enjoy it on the way down.

Roland Carter, US pole-vaulter

It's only jumping into a sandpit.

Jonathan Edwards, British Olympic triple jumper, on his world record triple jump

---

If this new method is accepted I will personally break my javelin in half and use it as a support for my tomato plants.

Dana Zatopekova, US Olympic javelin thrower, on news of a new throwing style

Plainly no way has yet been found
to stop long-jump commentaries
sounding like naughty stories after
lights-out in the dorm – 'Ooooh!
It's enormous. It was so long!'

Russell Davies, radio commentator

———•———

I always wanted to be a minor poet.
I remember when I did my record
long jump saying to myself, when
I was in the air half-way, 'This
may be pretty good jumping. It's
dashed poor minor poetry!'

**C. B. Fry, British cricket player and
Olympic athlete (1872–1956)**

———•———

I know I'm no Kim Basinger,
but she can't throw a javelin.

Fatima Whitbread, British Olympic javelin thrower

I don't think the discus will ever attract any interest until they let us start throwing them at one another.

Al Oerter, US Olympic discus thrower

As a runner Daley Thompson
is excellent, as a jumper he is
excellent, and as a thrower he is
an excellent runner and jumper.

Cliff Temple, sportswriter

———•———

Behind every good decathlete,
there's a good doctor.

Bill Toomey, US Olympic decathlete and commentator

———•———

The decathlon is nine Mickey
Mouse events and the 1500 metres.

Steve Ovett, British Olympic middle distance runner

When I lost my decathlon world
record I took it like a man. I
only cried for ten hours.

Daley Thompson, British Olympic decathlete

———◆———

We do not have cross-country
and we do not have pole-vaulting.

Gerald Curtin on Sing-Sing Prison's athletics day

———◆———

If Diane Modahl was 40 times
over the testosterone limit she'd
have a deep voice and we'd all
be calling her Barry White.

Tony Jarrett, British sprint and hurdling athlete

———◆———

The 880-yard heel and toe walk
is the closest a man can come to
experiencing the pangs of childbirth.

**Avery Brundage, US decathlete and
sports official (1887–1975)**

You have to be
suspicious when you
line up against girls
with moustaches.

Maree Holland, Australian Olympic sprinter

Baseball and Softball

In the great department store of life, baseball is the toy department.

Unknown

———

A hot dog at the ball park is better than a steak at the Ritz.

Humphrey Bogart, US actor (1899–1957)

———

You teach me baseball and I'll teach you relativity... No we must not – you will learn about relativity faster than I learn baseball.

Albert Einstein (1879–1955)

Baseball has the great advantage
over cricket of being ended sooner.

George Bernard Shaw, Irish literary critic,
playwright and essayist (1856–1950)

If [a woman] had to choose
between catching a fly ball and
saving an infant's life, she would
probably elect to save the infant's
life, without even considering
whether there were men on base.

Dave Barry, US writer and humorist

*On the notion that pitching is 90%
mental and only 10% physical –*

If that was true, then I'd be soaking my head in this bucket.

Tug McGraw, baseball pitcher, while soaking
his arm in a bucket of ice after a game

The difference between politics
and baseball is that in baseball when
you get caught stealing, you're out.

Ron Dentinger, US comedian

———•———

You gotta be a man to play
baseball for a living, but you gotta
have a lot of little boy in you too.

Roy Campanella, US baseball player (1921–1993)

———•———

Don't look back. Something
might be gaining on you.

Leroy 'Satchel' Paige, US baseball
player (1906–1982)

Smile well and often. It makes
people wonder what you're up to.

Leroy 'Satchel' Paige

———•———

Baseball hasn't been the national
pastime for many years now – no
sport is. The national pastime, like
it or not, is watching television.

Bob Greene, US health expert

If it weren't for
baseball, many kids
wouldn't know what a
millionaire looked like.

Phyllis Diller, US comedienne

With the money I'm making, I should be playing two positions.

Pete Rose, US baseball player

The difference between the old ball player and the new ball player is the jersey. The old ball player cared about the name on the front. The new ball player cares about the name on the back.

Steve Garvey, US baseball player

A great catch is like watching girls go by; the last one you see is always the prettiest.

Bob Gibson, US baseball player

Basketball

This is the second most exciting indoor sport, and the other one shouldn't have spectators.

Dick Vertleib, US basketball coach

I'm not a big sports fan, but I love it when they 'slam dunk'. That's sexy.

Emma Bunton, British singer

There are two kinds of coaches – those who have been fired and those who will be fired.

Ken Loeffler, basketball coach

Shooting is just like toenails. They may fall off occasionally, but you know they'll always come back.

Charles Johnson, basketball player

If cocaine were helium, the NBA would float away.

Art Rust, sports commentator and historian

The game is too long, the season is too long and the players are too long.

Jack Dolph, American Basketball Association

I told one player,
'Son, I couldn't
understand it with
you. Is it ignorance
or apathy?' He said,
'Coach, I don't know
and I don't care.'

Frank Layden, US basketball coach

I'm in favour of drug tests, just so long as they are multiple choice.

Kurt Rambis, basketball coach

———◆———

If the NBA were on Channel 5 and a bunch of frogs making love was on Channel 4, I'd watch the frogs, even if they were coming in fuzzy.

Bobby Knight, US basketball coach

———◆———

I liked the choreography, but I didn't care for the costumes.

Tommy Tune, actor, dancer and singer, on why he never considered playing basketball

The secret is to have eight
great players and four others
who will cheer like crazy.

Jerry Tarkanian, US basketball coach

———◆———

I hate it. It looks like a stick-up
at 7-Eleven. Five guys standing
there with their hands in the air.

Norm Sloan, US basketball coach
(1926–2003), on zone defence

Fans never fall
asleep at our games,
because they're
afraid they might
get hit by a pass.

George Raveling, US basketball coach

Boxing

It's just a job. Grass grows,
birds fly, waves pound the
sand. I just beat people up.
Muhammad Ali, US boxer, nicknamed 'The Greatest'

It's hard to be humble, when
you're as great as I am.
Muhammad Ali

Boxers, who thrive in a cruel,
unnatural sporting world, fight each
other harder with words and insults
before a bout than they may do
in the ring. It is good publicity.
Jack Fingleton, British cricket player (1908–1981)

My girlfriend boos me when
we make love because she
knows it turns me on.

Hector Camacho, Puerto Rican boxer

The bigger they are the
harder they fall.

Bob Fitzsimmons, British boxer (1863–1917)

I want to keep fighting because
it is the only thing that keeps
me out of hamburger joints. If I
don't fight, I'll eat this planet.

George Foreman

Boxing is a little like jazz. The better it is the fewer people can understand it.

George Foreman, US boxer

If I miss the guy with the left and
the right, I belly-bump him.

George Foreman

Seems everyone I've fought
had a secret punch but I
never got to see it.

Bob Foster, US boxer

The noble science of boxing is all
our own. Foreigners can scarcely
understand how we can squeeze
pleasure out of this pastime; the
luxury of hard blows given or
received; the joy of the ring; nor the
perseverance of the combatants.

William Hazlitt, essayist (1778–1830), *Merry England*

It was a very happy fight. I
was enjoying hitting him and
he enjoyed getting hit.

Lennox Lewis, British boxer

The constant use of those surest
keepers of the peace, the boxing
gloves, kept the School-house
boys from fighting one another.

Thomas Hughes, novelist (1822–1896),
Tom Brown's Schooldays

I call it my check-hook, I check to
see if he's there, then I throw it.

Roy Jones Jr., US boxer

Boxing's a great
soap opera but
at the moment it's
Coronation Street
without balls and
I want it to be
Dallas with balls.

Barry Hearn, boxing manager

A boxing match is like a cowboy
movie. There's got to be good
guys and there's got to be bad
guys. That's what the people pay
for, to see the bad guys get beat.

Sonny Liston, US boxer (1932–1970)

I knew how to beat Rocky
[Marciano]. Just jab, jab, jab
and cross a right. Rocky was
insulted if you missed him.

Joe Louis, US boxer (1914–1981)

I figured that if I said it enough,
I would convince the world that
I really was the greatest.

Muhammad Ali

Talking and bragging made me fight better. I had to back up what I said.

Muhammad Ali

In his prime, Bugnor had the physique of a Greek statue, but he had fewer moves.

Hugh McIlvanney, sportswriter and commentator

Once in the ring, it don't matter how many people are watching. They won't be able to help.

Terry Marsh, British boxer

Boxing is probably
the best and most
individual lifestyle
you can have without
being a criminal.

Randy Neumann, US boxer

Boxing has... immense value. It teaches you never – that it is a disaster – to lose your temper, that there can be great nobility in losing, that fear lies in the heart and mind and that skill will always beat might.

Lord Morris, politician

Boxing is the best job in the world to let off steam, and people are in trouble when Tyson wants to let off steam.

Michael Spinks, US boxer

OK, I'm the youngest ever heavyweight champion: my only ambition now is to be the oldest.

Mike Tyson, US boxer

Nothing is going to stop Tyson
that doesn't have a motor attached.

David Brenner, comedian

So far as I know, the brain
has no way of distinguishing a
blow from a professional from
a blow from an amateur.

**Lord Brain, (1895–1966) on a bill to
prohibit professional boxing**

If they can make penicillin out
of mouldy bread, they can sure
make something out of you.

Muhammad Ali

I don't mind the
title fight going
out at three in the
morning. Everyone
in Glasgow fights at
three in the morning.

Jim Watt, British boxer

The man who views the world at
50 the same as he did at 20 has
wasted 30 years of his life.

Muhammad Ali

———

May the day never come when an
Englishman shall feel ashamed
of it (boxing), or blackguards
bring it to a disgrace.

John Broughton, British boxer (1705–1789)

———

Silence is golden when you
can't think of a good answer.

Muhammad Ali

If you screw things up in tennis,
it's 15-love. If you screw up
in boxing, it's your ass.

Randall 'Tex' Cobb, US heavyweight boxer

———————

I was called 'Rembrandt' Hope in
my boxing days, because I spent
so much time on the canvas.

Bob Hope

———————

He has turned defensive boxing
into a poetic art. Trouble
is nobody ever knocked
anybody out with a poem.

**Eddie Shaw, Northern Irish boxing coach,
referring to Herol 'Bomber' Graham**

I've seen George
Foreman shadow
boxing and the
shadow won.

Muhammad Ali

Baroness: Mr Cooper, have you looked in the mirror lately and seen the state of your nose? Cooper: Well madam, have you looked in the mirror and seen the state of your nose? Boxing is my excuse. What's yours?

Henry Cooper, British heavyweight boxer, replying to boxing abolitionist Baroness Edith Summerskill about the brutalities of the sport

---

Don't make me laugh! It's the WBF belt – I heard they are giving them away with five litres of petrol down at Texaco.

Herbie Hide, British boxer, reacting to the news that Audley Harrison has won the world WBF heavyweight title

---

I'm so quick, I can click off the light and be in bed before the room gets dark.

Muhammad Ali

If anyone even dreams he
beat me, he had better
wake up and apologise.

Muhammad Ali

With every punch that I am
throwing at Harrison, I will imagine
the face of Malcolm Glazer and
that will be enough motivation
for me to win the world title.

**Boxer and Manchester United fan Michael Brodie
before losing his fight with Scott Harrison**

He's gonna need an industrial-strength toothpick to pick the leather out of his teeth. I'm gonna hit this man so hard he's gonna grow an Afro.

Michael Olajide, US boxer, on fighting Iran Berkley

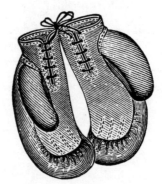

George Chuvalo's best punch is
a left cheek to the right glove.

Larry Merchant, boxing analysist and commentator

I fought Sugar [Ray Robinson]
so many times that I'm lucky
I didn't get diabetes.

Jake 'Raging Bull' LaMotta, US boxer and actor

There are certain things
you can't get back, like the
elastic in your socks.

**Eddie Futch, US boxer (1911–2001),
on boxing comebacks**

I'm going to say hello to two friends who I've shut out of my life for the past ten weeks while I trained the hardest I've ever done for a fight. So welcome back Mr Guinness and Mr Dom Perignon.

Ricky Hatton, British boxer

I used to nick suits for a living, now I pay a grand for them.

Chris Eubank, British boxer

Boxing is a great exercise... as long as you can yell 'cut' whenever you want to.

Sylvester Stallone, US actor

To me, boxing is like a ballet, except there's no music, no choreography, and the dancers hit each other.

Jack Handey, comedian and comic writer

Prize fighters can sometimes read
and write when they start – but
they can't when they finish.

Martin H. Fischer, scientist (1879–1962)

For ageing boxers, first your
legs go. Then your reflexes
go, then your friends go.

Willie Pep, US boxer

Cricket

It's a funny kind of month, October. For the really keen cricket fan it's when you discover that your wife left you in May.

Denis Norden, comedy writer, TV personality

———•———

I'm confident they play the game in heaven. Wouldn't be heaven otherwise, would it?

Patrick Moore, astronomer, on cricket

———•———

I tend to believe that cricket is the greatest thing that God ever created on earth... certainly greater than sex, although sex isn't too bad either.

Harold Pinter, playwright

Personally, I have always looked
on cricket as organised loafing.

**William Temple, Ninth Archbishop
of Canterbury (1881–1944)**

It's not in support of cricket but as
an earnest protest against golf.

**Max Beerbohm, critic, essayist and
caricaturist (1872–1956), when asked to
contribute to W. G. Grace's testimonial**

It's hard work making
batting look effortless.

David Gower, British cricket player

I bowl so slow
that if after I have
delivered the ball I
don't like the look
of it, I can run after
it and bring it back.

J. M. Barrie, Scottish novelist and
playwright (1860–1937)

Fast bowling isn't hard
work, it's horse work.

Fred Trueman, British cricket player

———

They came to see me bat
not to see you bowl.

**W. G. Grace, British cricket player (1848–
1915), on refusing to leave the crease
having been bowled out by the first ball**

———

Cricket is full of glorious
chances, and the Goddess who
presides over it loves to bring
down the most skilful player.

Thomas Hughes, *Tom Brown's Schooldays*

CRICKET

You know Lord's? Well, once I played there
And a ball I hit to leg
Struck the umpire's head, stayed there
As a nest retains an egg.

Harry Graham, writer (1874–1936), *Ruthless Rhymes*

———•———

You should play every game
as if it's your last, but make
sure you perform well enough
to ensure that it's not.

John Embury, British cricket player

———•———

There's no more amateurish
professional game in the world.

John Embury

Cricket is certainly
a very good and
wholesome exercise,
yet it may be abused
if either great or
little people make
it their business.

Gentleman's Magazine, 1743

You are only as good
as your last game.

Ian Botham, British cricket player

———•———

Cowans should remember what
happened to Graham Dilley, who
started out as a genuinely quick
bowler. They started stuffing
'line and length' into his ear, and
now he has Dennis Lillee's action
with Dennis Thatcher's pace.

Geoff Boycott, British cricket player

———•———

If you can't always play
like a cricketer, you can
at least look like one.

**Sir Donald Bradman, Australian
cricket player (1908–2001)**

When we were children we asked
my Uncle Charles what it was like
to play cricket with W. G. Grace.
'The dirtiest neck I ever kept
wicket behind,' was his crisp reply.

Lord Chandos

If I'd done a quarter of the things
of which I'm accused, I'd be pickled
in alcohol. I'd be a registered
drug addict and would have sired
half the children in the world's
cricket-playing countries.

Ian Botham

I have been to many functions
where some great cricketers of
the past have been present. To
see some of them sink their drink
is to witness performances as
awe-inspiring as ever any of them
displayed on the cricket field.

Ian Botham

Nothing yet devised
by man is worse for
a sick hangover than
a day's cricket in
the summer sun.

Michael Parkinson, TV personality

What is both surprising and delightful is that spectators are allowed, and even expected, to join in the vocal part of the game... There is no reason why the field should not try to put the batsman off his stroke at the critical moment by neatly timed disparagements of his wife's fidelity and his mother's respectability.

George Bernard Shaw

Oh God! If there be cricket in heaven let there also be rain.

Alec Douglas-Home, politician (1903–1995)

In my opinion cricket is too great a game to think about statistically.

E. H. Hendren, British cricketer (1889–1962)

It requires one to assume
such indecent postures.

Oscar Wilde, writer (1854–1900)

Cricket is the only game
that you can actually put
on weight when playing.

Tommy Docherty, football pundit

Maybe it's that tally-ho
attitude. You know, there'll
always be an England, all that
Empire crap they dish out.
But I never could cop Poms.

Jeff Thomson, Australian cricket player

If the Poms bat
first, let's tell the
taxi to wait.

Australian fans' banner (1995)

England will win if Camilla Parker bowls.

Australian fans' banner (1995)

———•———

I've done the elephant. I've done the poverty. I might as well go home.

Phil Tufnell, British cricket player, during England's tour of India

———•———

On being asked what he looked forward to most upon returning from a long tour of India –

A dry fart!

Phil Edmonds, British cricket player

I just want to get into the middle
and get the right sort of runs.

**Robin Smith, South African cricket player, on
suffering from diarrhoea on tour in India**

———— ·—·—— ————

I want to play cricket, it doesn't
seem to matter if you win or lose.

Meat Loaf, US singer

David Gower: Do
you want Gatting
a foot wider?
Chris Cowdrey:
No. He'd burst.

During the 1985 India v England Test in Calcutta

It would be extremely difficult for me to choose between singing Elvis Presley songs and scoring a century for England, but I think I would choose a century for England.

Tim Rice, lyricist, radio presenter and author

To the moustached Dennis Lillee –

Are you aware, Sir, that the last time I saw anything like that on a top lip, the whole herd had to be destroyed?

Eric Morecambe, British comedian (1926–1984)

This bowler's like my dog: three short legs and balls that swing each way.

Brian Johnston, British cricket commentator (1912–1994)

CRICKET

A snick by Jack Hobbs is a sort of disturbance of a cosmic orderliness.

Sir Neville Cardus, cricket writer (1889–1975)

Denis Compton was the only player to call his partner for a run and wish him good luck at the same time.

John Warr, British cricket player

Ken Harrington: Let's cut out some of the quick singles.
Fred Titmus: OK! We'll cut out yours, Ken.

During a mid-wicket conference in a Test match

I can't really say I'm batting badly. I'm not batting long enough to be batting badly.

Greg Chappell, Australian cricket player

I never wanted to make a hundred.
Who wants to make a hundred
anyway? When I first went in,
my immediate objective was to
hit the ball to each of the four
corners of the field. After that,
I tried not to be repetitive.

**Lord Learie Constantine, Tobagan-born
cricketer and political activist (1901–1971)**

---

*On the Kent batsman giving
Lancashire's Ian Austin the charge –*

Matthew Fleming used to be in the
Green Jackets, but the way he's
batting suggests he'd be better
suited in the Light Brigade.

Charles Colvite, sports commentator

It's like Manchester United
getting a penalty and Bryan
Robson taking it with his head.

**David Lloyd, British cricket player,
on the reverse sweep**

Sir Donald Bradman
Would have been a very glad man
If his Test average had been .06 more
Than 99.94.

T. N. E. Smith

I don't suppose I can call you a
lucky bleeder when you've got 347.

**Angus Fraser, British cricket player
and journalist, to Brian Lara**

The English are not very spiritual
people, so they invented cricket to
give them some idea of eternity.

George Bernard Shaw

Cricket is basically
baseball on valium.

Robin Williams, US actor

When's the game itself going to begin?

Groucho Marx, US actor (1895–1977),
whilst watching a cricket match at Lords

Fishing

There's a fine line between fishing and standing on the shore like an idiot.

Steven Wright, US comedian

Fishing seems to be divided, like sex, into three unequal parts: anticipation, recollection, and between them, actual performance.

Arnold Gingrich, US journalist (1903–1976)

Fly fishing may be a very pleasant amusement; but angling or float fishing I can only compare to a stick and a string, with a worm at one end and a fool at the other.

Samuel Johnson, British lexicographer and critic (1709–1784)

There is considerable talk about the most efficient colours to use in the angling process, whether one is using jigs or lures, spinners or harness. In this, there seems to be a bizarre connection to the world of fashion. Several years ago, it was accepted as fact that hungry pickerel were enamoured of anything chartreuse. As a result, men who until that point in their lives would have actually questioned the sexual orientation of anyone using the word 'chartreuse' were now tossing the word around like a Frisbee. One has to wonder how the fish manage to keep abreast of the latest fads, especially when the lack of sunlight at the depth of sixty or seventy feet pretty much makes one colour indiscernible from another anyway.

Brad Smith, Canadian writer, *Local Rules*

Golf

Golf is a good walk spoiled.

Mark Twain, US author (1835–1910)

If you watch a game, it's fun.
If you play it, it's recreation.
If you work at it, it's golf.

Bob Hope

Sudden success in golf is
like the sudden acquisition of
wealth. It is apt to unsettle and
deteriorate the character.

P. G. Wodehouse, British comic writer (1881–1975)

The place of the father
in the modern suburban
family is a very small one,
particularly if he plays golf.

**Bertrand Russell, British philosopher, logician
and Nobel Prize winner (1872–1970)**

I've got the drinkers and the
smokers and the eaters on my
side. They like what we do.

John Daly, golfer

Golf is a game in which you can
claim the privileges of age and
retain the playthings of childhood.

**Samuel Johnson, critic, poet
and essayist (1649–1703)**

Golf is a day
spent in a round of
strenuous idleness.

William Wordsworth, poet and essayist (1770–1850)

Golf is a game whose aim it is to hit a very small ball into an even smaller hole with weapons singularly ill-designed for the purpose.

Winston Churchill (1874–1965)

Golf is very much like a love affair; if you don't take it seriously, it's no fun; if you do, it breaks your heart. Don't break your heart, but flirt with the possibility.

Louise Suggs, US golfer

Reverse every natural instinct and do the opposite of what you are inclined to do, and you will probably come very close to having a perfect golf swing.

Ben Hogan, US golfer (1912–1997)

Playing the US Open is like
tippy-toeing through hell.

Jerry McGee, US golfer

Eighteen holes of match or medal
play will teach you more about
your foe than will eighteen years
of dealing with him across a desk.

Grantland Rice, US sportswriter (1880–1954)

I know I'm getting better because
I'm hitting fewer spectators.

Gerald Ford, former US president

If you think it's hard
to meet new people,
try picking up the
wrong golf ball.

Jack Lemmon, US comedy actor (1925–2001)

It's good sportsmanship to
not pick up lost golf balls
while they are still rolling.

Mark Twain

———•———

The hardest shot is the chip at
90 yards from the green where
the ball has to be played against
an oak tree, bounces back into a
sandtrap, hits a stone, bounces
onto the green, and then rolls
into the cup. That shot is so
difficult I have only made it once.

Zeppo Marx, US comedy actor (1901–1979)

Hockey is a sport for white men. Basketball is a sport for black men. Golf is a sport for white men dressed like pimps.

Tiger Woods, US golfer

Golf is good for the soul. You get so mad at yourself you forget to hate your enemies.

Will Rogers, US performer and journalist (1879–1935)

It's not whether you win or lose – but whether I win or lose.

Sandy Lyle, British golfer

Golf and sex are
about the only things
you can enjoy without
being good at.

Jimmy Demaret, US golfer

Go play golf. Go to the golf course. Hit the ball. Find the ball. Repeat until the ball is in the hole. Have fun. The end.

Chuck Hogan, US golf instructor

Retire to what? I'm a golfer and a fisherman. I've got no place to retire to.

Julius Boros, US golfer (1920–1994)

I'm working as hard as I can to get my life and my cash to run out at the same time. If I can just die after lunch Tuesday, everything would be perfect.

Doug Sanders, US golfer

My favourite shots are the practice
swing and the conceded putt.
The rest can never be mastered.

Lord Robertson, politician

It took me seventeen years to get
three thousand hits in baseball. I
did it in one afternoon playing golf.

Henry Aaron, US baseball player

They called it golf
because all the
other four letter
words were taken.

Walter Hagen, US golfer and professional
golf pioneer (1892–1969)

Golf was once a rich
man's sport, but now it has
millions of poor players.

Unknown

———•———

Golfers are the greatest
worriers in the world of sport.

Billy Casper, US golfer

———•———

It's not just enough to swing at
the ball. You've got to loosen
your girdle and let 'er fly.

Babe Didrikson Zaharias, US golfer (1914–1956)

Golf balls are attracted to water as unerringly as the eye of a middle-aged man to a female bosom.

Michael Green, British humorist

Ice Hockey

They say atomic radiation can
hurt your reproductive organs. My
answer is, so can a hockey stick.
But we don't stop building them.

Johnny Carson, US TV host

I went to a fight the other night
and a hockey game broke out.

Rodney Dangerfield, US comedian
and actor (1921–2004)

A puck is a hard rubber disc
that hockey players strike when
they can't hit one another.

Jimmy Cannon, US sportswriter, (1910–1973)

Ice hockey is a form of disorderly conduct in which the score is kept.

Doug Larson, US writer

———•———

If you take the game seriously, you go crazy anyway, so it helps if you're a bit nuts to start with because you don't waste time getting that way.

Bob Plager, US ice hockey player

How would you like
a job where, every
time you make a
mistake, a big red
light goes on and
18,000 people boo?

Jacques Plante, Canadian ice
hockey player (1929–1986)

Horse Racing

Nobody ever bet enough
on a winning horse.

Richard Sasuly, author

———•———

Money, horse racing and
women, three things the boys
just can't figure out.

Will Rogers, American entertainer (1879–1935)

———•———

Riding is the art of keeping a horse
between yourself and the ground.

Anonymous

Horse racing is animated roulette.

Roger Kahn, US sports writer

After one of them has won the Kentucky Derby, any breeding expert can sit down and show you just why he won – from his pedigree. The only trouble is, the expert can't do it before the race.

Phil Chinn, Kentucky horse trader

I know nothing about racing and any money I put on a horse is a sort of insurance policy to prevent it winning.

Frank Richardson, actor

One way to stop
a runaway horse
is to bet on him.

Jeffrey Bernard, British journalist (1932–1997)

A bookie is just a pickpocket who lets you use your own hands.

Henry Morgan, US actor

Sex is an anti-climax after that!

Mark Fitzgerald, Grand National winning jockey

There is little to compare with the thrill of standing next to the creature in the winner's enclosure avoiding his hooves and receiving the congratulations of the press, your trainer and friends who backed it. What makes the experience so satisfying is that you, the owner, have had absolutely nothing to do with the horse winning.

Robert Morley, British actor (1908–1992)

I have no intention of watching
undersized Englishmen perched
on horses with matchstick legs
race along courses planned
to amuse Nell Gwynn.

Gilbert Harding, British journalist (1907–1960)

A loose horse is any horse
sensible enough to get rid of
its rider at an early stage and
carry on unencumbered.

Clive James, Australian writer and critic

There are, they say,
fools, bloody fools,
and men who remount
in a steeplechase.

John Oaksey, British sports commentator and jockey

Motor Racing

You win some, you lose
some, you wreck some.

Dale Earnhardt, US racing driver (1951–2001)

———

I think NASCAR would
be much more exciting if, like
in a skating rink, every fifteen
minutes someone announced it
was time to reverse direction.

Jeffrey T. Anbinder, US writer

———

If you wait, all that happens
is that you get older.

Mario Andretti, Italian racing driver

I couldn't find the sports car of
my dreams, so I built it myself.

Dr. Ferdinand Porsche (1875–1951)

———————

My brother is crazy... sometimes
he's just not right in the head!

**Ralf Schumacher, German racing driver,
after brother Michael nearly forced him off
the track at the Monaco Grand Prix**

———————

I'm a full-blooded racer, that's why
I'm here – not for a Sunday outing.

Michael Schumacher, German racing driver

If everything is under
control, you are
going too slow.

Mario Andretti

I don't make mistakes. I make prophecies which immediately turn out to be wrong.

Murray Walker, motor sports commentator

———•———

I'm not a big milk drinker. But for once it tasted great!

Dan Wheldon, British racing driver, after winning America's prestigious Indy 500 and getting the traditional prize of a pint of milk

———•———

At 180 mph, when your front wheel wants to play pogo stick, you don't do nothing. You don't sneeze, you don't hiccup, you don't even breathe. All you do is point it and hang on.

Kenny Roberts, US racing driver

It is necessary to relax your
muscles when you can.
Relaxing your brain is fatal.

Stirling Moss, British racing driver

On the dangers of the Monte Carlo Rally –
Some of the ravines are so deep
that if you topple over, your
clothes will be out of date by
the time you hit the bottom.

Tony Pond, British rally driver

Grand Prix driving is like
balancing an egg on a spoon
while shooting the rapids.

Graham Hill, British racing driver (1929–1975)

Racing is 99 per
cent boredom and
one per cent terror.

Geoff Brabham, Australian racing driver

You drive the car, you don't carry it.

Janet Guthrie, US racing driver, on
being asked if female drivers were as
strong as their male counterparts

There are only two things no
man will admit he can't do well:
drive a car and make love.

Stirling Moss

Refs And Umpires

You can say something to popes,
kings and presidents, but you can't
talk to officials. In the next war they
ought to give everyone a whistle.

Abe Lemmons

———•———

I wanted to have a career in sports
when I was young, but I had to
give it up. I'm only six feet tall,
so I couldn't play basketball. I'm
only 190 pounds, so I couldn't
play football. And I have 20-20
vision, so I couldn't be a referee.

Jay Leno

———•———

The umpire... is like the geyser
in the bathroom; we cannot
do without it, yet we notice it
only when it is out of order.

Neville Cardus, cricket writer (1889–1975)

We're supposed to be perfect
our first day on the job, and then
show constant improvement.

Ed Vargo, baseball umpire

———◆———

I cannot for the life of me see why
the umpires, the only two people
on a cricket field who are not
going to get grass stains on their
knees, are the only two people
allowed to wear dark trousers.

Katherine Whitehorn, journalist

———◆———

The first half is invariably much
longer than the second. This
is partly because of the late
kick-off but is also caused by
the unfitness of the referee.

Michael Green, British humorist,
The Art of Coarse Rugby

I think you enjoy the
game more if you
don't know the rules.
Anyway, you're on
the same wavelength
as the referees.

Jonathan Davies, British rugby player, on rugby

We don't need refs, but I guess
white guys need something to do.

Charles Barkley, basketball player

A baseball fan is a spectator
sitting 500 feet from home plate...
who can see better than an
umpire standing five feet away.

Unknown

The trouble with referees is that
they just don't care which side wins.

Tom Canterbury

I never comment on referees
and I'm not going to break the
habit of a lifetime for that prat.

Norman Whiteside, football player

Grandmother or tails, sir?

**Anon rugby referee to Princess Anne's son Peter
Phillips, for his pre-match coin-toss preference**

The Sporting Life

The genius of the British lends
itself not so much to the winning
of games as to their invention. An
astonishing number of international
games were invented by the
British, who, whenever they are
surpassed by other nations, coolly
invent another one which they
can dominate for a while by being
the only ones to know the rules.

Peter Ustinov, *Dear Me*

So frivolous is [Man] that, though
full of a thousand reasons for
weariness, the least thing, such as
playing billiards or hitting a ball, is
sufficient enough to amuse him.

Blaise Pascal, French mathematician (1623–1662)

I always turn to the sports pages
first, which record people's
accomplishments. The front page
has nothing but man's failures.

Chief Justice Earl Warren (1891–1974)

The more violent the body
contact of the sports you
watch, the lower your class.

Paul Fussell, US author

Sports is the only entertainment
where, no matter how many
times you go back, you
never know the ending.

Neil Simon, US playwright

Sports do not build
character. They reveal it.

John Wooden, basketball coach

I'm not a yeller. My theory is that no one goes out there trying to screw up.

Amy Ruley, basketball coach

I hate all sports as rabidly
as a person who likes sports
hates common sense.

Henry Louis Mencken, US journalist
and critic (1880–1956)

The more you sweat in practice,
the less you bleed in battle.

Unknown

Every sport pretends to a
literature, but people don't believe
it of any other sport but their own.

Sir Alistair Cooke, journalist and
commentator (1908–2004)

People understand contests. You take a bunch of kids throwing rocks at random and people look askance, but if you go and hold a rock-throwing contest – people understand that.

Don Murray, US actor

———•———

In the field of sports you are more or less accepted for what you do rather than what you are.

Althea Gibson, US tennis player (1927–2003)

Years ago we discovered the exact point, the dead centre of middle age. It occurs when you are too young to take up golf and too old to rush up to the net.

Franklin P. Adams, US journalist and
radio personality (1881–1960)

If all the year were playing holidays
To sport would be as
tedious as to work.

**William Shakespeare, poet and playwright
(1564–1616)** *Henry IV, Part I*

You can discover more about a
person in an hour of play than
in a year of conversation.

Plato (427–347 BC)

The breakfast of champions is
not cereal, it's the opposition.

Nick Seitz, golf writer

It is a noteworthy fact that kicking and beating have played so considerable a part in the habits which necessity has imposed on mankind in past ages, that the only way of preventing civilised men from beating and kicking their wives is to organise games in which they can kick and beat balls.

George Bernard Shaw

If you make every game a life-and-death thing, you're going to have problems.

Dean Smith, basketball coach

Pain is weakness leaving the body.

Tom Sobol, World Snowshoe Racing Champion

Depend on the
rabbit's foot if you
will, but remember
it didn't work for
the rabbit.

R. E. Shay, author

I must complain the cards are ill
shuffled till I have a good hand.

Jonathan Swift, Anglo-Irish satirist, poet and essayist
(1667–1745), from *Thoughts on Various Subjects*

Luck is what happens when
preparation meets opportunity.

Darrel Royal, American football coach

Adversity causes some men to
break; others to break records.

William A. Ward, US college
administrator (1921–1994)

A day for toil, an hour for sport,
but for a friend is life too short.

**Ralph Waldo Emerson, US philosopher,
poet and essayist (1803–1882)**

——•——

Have you noticed that whatever
sport you're trying to learn, some
earnest person is always telling
you to keep your knees bent?

Dave Barry

——•——

As I understand it, sport is hard
work for which you do not get paid.

Irvin S. Cobb, US journalist and humorist (1876–1944)

There are no
traffic jams along
the extra mile.

Roger Staubach, American football player

If only Hitler and Mussolini could
have a good game of bowls once a
week at Geneva, I feel that Europe
would not be as troubled as it is.

R. G. Briscow, British politician (1893–1957)

It is foolish and quite unfitting for
an educated man to spend all his
time on acquiring bulging muscles, a
thick neck and mighty thighs. The
large amounts they are compelled
to eat make them dull-witted.

Seneca (4 BC–65 AD)

One day of practice is like
one day of clean living. It
doesn't do you any good.

Abe Lemmons

———•———

I don't care for sex. I find it an
embarrassing, dull exercise. I
prefer sports, where you can win.

Norm Macdonald, Canadian actor

Black people dominate sports in the United States. Twenty per cent of the population and ninety per cent of the final four. We own this shit. Basketball, baseball, football, golf, tennis, and as soon as they make a heated hockey rink we'll take that shit too.

Chris Rock, US actor

To brag little – to
show well – to crow
gently if in luck
– to pay up, to
own up, and to
shut up if beaten,
are the virtues of
a sporting man.

Oliver Wendell Holmes, US physician,
poet and humorist (1809–1894)

Rugby

In 1823, William Webb Ellis
first picked up the ball in his
arms and ran with it. And for the
next 156 years forwards have
been trying to work out why.

Sir Tasker Watkins, Victoria Cross recipient and
former president of the Welsh Rugby Union

Modern rugby players... like to
get their retaliation in first.

Kim Fletcher, Australian writer

Rugby League is much, much
more physical than Rugby
Union, and that's before anyone
starts breaking the rules.

Adrian Hadley, Welsh rugby player

Players in secure employment
and happily married are
always more consistent than
the young tearaways.

Dusty Hare, British rugby player

They came to a sort of gigantic
gallows of two poles eighteen
feet high, fixed upright in the
ground some fourteen feet apart
with a cross-bar running from
one to the other at the height
of ten feet or thereabouts.

Thomas Hughes, *Tom Brown's Schooldays*

There is far too much talk about
good ball and bad ball. In my
opinion, good ball is when you
have possession and bad ball is
when the opposition have it.

Dick Jeeps, rugby player

This sport is
supposed to be
about controlled
aggression; perhaps
I just control mine
better than most.

Roy Powell, politician (1928–2001)

I love what rugby is – brain
as well as braun, and then
beer together afterwards.

Roy Laidlaw, British rugby player

Backs are the poets in motion
of rugby, and all the excitement
occurs when they are engaged.

Russell Celyn Jones, journalist

[Forwards are] like boxers,
like rutting stags.

Ray Prosser, Welsh rugby player and coach

Dirty play should never be condoned. Nor should softness.

John Scott, Welsh rugby columnist

That's the amazing thing about team games; you can play in a match against your best mate and with a total stranger. But for that eighty minutes the total stranger is your very best mate in the world and your lifelong friend becomes the enemy.

Brian Smith, Australian rugby coach

We're serious and we are social. That's part of what's so great about rugby.

Raul Socher, US rugby player

We'll probably drink
as hard as we train
– that's very hard.
Stuart Barnes, British rugby player

I thought I would have a quiet pint... and about 17 noisy ones.

Gareth Chilcott, British rugby player, on playing his last game of rugby for Bath.

Violence on the rugby field is a bore.

Denis Thatcher, businessman and husband of Margaret Thatcher, former British prime minister

---

Rugby is a good occasion for keeping thirty bullies far from the centre of the city.

Oscar Wilde

We've lost seven of our last eight matches. Only team that we've beaten was Western Samoa. Good job we didn't play the whole of Samoa.

Gareth Davies, British rugby player

———•———

In south west Lancashire, babes don't toddle, they side-step. Queuing women talk of 'nipping round the blindside'. Rugby League provides our cultural adrenalin. It's a physical manifestation of our rules of life, comradeship, honest endeavour, and a staunch, often ponderous allegiance to fair play.

Colin Welland, actor and television writer

Not many people in Batley speak Latin, so the first thing we did was change the motto.

Stephen Ball on taking over as Batley chairman

Playing rugby at school I once fell on a loose ball and, through ignorance and fear, held on despite a fierce pummelling. After that it took me months to convince my team-mates I was a coward.

Peter Cook, British satirist, writer and comedian (1937–1995)

Ray Gravell Eats Soft Centres.

Banner at Cardiff Arms Park (1970s)

Rugby is a game for the mentally deficient... That is why it was invented by the British. Who else but an Englishman could invent an oval ball?

Peter Pook, comedy writer, *Pook's Love Nest*

[The ball] is specially shaped like
a lozenge so it cannot roll, bounce
properly or do any of the things
for which a ball was designed.

Stephen Pile, British writer

———

Rugby is played by men
with odd-shaped balls.

Car bumper sticker

The advantage law is the best law in rugby, because it lets you ignore all the others for the good of the game.

Derek Robinson, British writer

Running

I became a great runner because
if you're a kid in Leeds and your
name is Sebastian you've got
to become a great runner.

Sebastian Coe, British middle distance runner

———•———

World records are only borrowed.

Sebastian Coe

———•———

If you want to win a race you
have to go a little berserk.

Bill Rodgers, American distance runner

There is a theory that if you enjoy
cross-country running you can
thrive on almost any kind of pain.

Peter Hildreth, British hurdle athlete

Running for money doesn't make
you run fast. It makes you run first.

Ben Jipcho, Kenyan distance runner

Naturally, we wanted to achieve
the honour of doing it first,
but the main essence of sport
is a race against opponents
rather than against clocks.

Roger Bannister, British track athlete (having run
a mile in less than four minutes on 6 May 1954)

If you want to know what you'll look like in ten years, look in the mirror after you've run a marathon.

Jeff Scaff, distance runner

Don't talk about Michael
Johnson's style. Look, if that
guy ran with his fingers up his bum
he could still run 42 seconds.

Roger Black, British 400m runner

I'm just a girl who runs.

Zola Budd, South African distance runner

Skiing

I really lack the words to
compliment myself today.
Alberto Tomba, Italian skier

I now realise that the small hills you
see on ski slopes are formed around
the bodies of forty-seven-year-olds
who tried to learn snowboarding.
Dave Barry

Skiing: the art of catching cold and
going broke while rapidly heading
nowhere at great personal risk.
Unknown

All things are possible, except for
skiing through a revolving door.
Unknown

If you're looking for a vacation
concept that combines the
element of outdoor fun with the
element of potentially knocking
down a tree with your face, you
can't do better than skiing.
Dave Barry

There are 206 bones
in the human body,
but don't worry. The
two in the middle
ear have never been
broken while skiing.

Unknown

Snooker, Pool and Billiards

Bums play pool, gentlemen play billiards.

Daniel McGoorty, US writer (1901–1970)

I have not come to Sheffield to look at the gardens near the hotel. If I didn't think I could win the World Championship I would go and play golf badly in Spain.

Jimmy White, British snooker player, on his chances of winning the World Championship

Maybe I should put myself forward for *I'm a Celebrity Get Me Out of Here!*. Then again, all the other guests would leave.

Alex Higgins, former snooker player,
thinking of ways to make a comeback

Someone threw a petrol bomb at Alex Higgins once and he drank it.

Frank Carson, comedian

Whoever called
snooker 'chess
with balls' was
rude, but right.

Clive James

Tennis

Never discuss love with a tennis player, it means nothing to them.

Unknown

———•———

Tennis is a perfect combination of violent action taking place in an atmosphere of total tranquillity.

Billie Jean King, US tennis player

———•———

Monica Seles: I'd hate to be next door to her on her wedding night.

Peter Ustinov, British actor and writer (1921–2004)

Michael Chang has all the fire and passion of a public service announcement, so much so that he makes Pete Sampras appear fascinating.

Alex Ramsey

I threw the kitchen sink at him but he went to the bathroom and came back with the tub.

Andy Roddick, US tennis player

When I was 40, my doctor advised me that a man in his 40s shouldn't play tennis. I heeded his advice carefully and could hardly wait until I reached 50 to start again.

Hugo Black, US politician and supreme court justice (1886–1971)

The depressing
thing about tennis is
that no matter how
good I get, I'll never
be as good as a wall.

Mitch Hedberg, US comedian (1968–2005)

You've got to win in sports – that's talent – but you've also got to learn how to remind everybody how you did win, and how often. That comes with experience.

Billie Jean King

When the Williams sisters play tennis, it gets pretty hot. When they start grunting, I'm in.

Robin Williams

My theory is that if you buy an ice-cream cone and make it hit your mouth, you can play. If you stick it on your forehead, your chances are less.

Vic Braden, US tennis coach

Why did I lose? No reason,
though you might like to know
that I got tired, my ears started
popping, the rubber came off
my shoes, I got cramp, and I lost
one of my contact lenses. Other
than that I was in great shape.

Bob Lutz, US tennis player

If someone says tennis is not
feminine, I say screw it.

Rosie Casals, US tennis player

If you're up against a girl with big boobs, bring her to the net, and make her hit backhand volleys. That's the hardest shot for the well endowed.

Billie Jean King

———•———

I'm not involved in tennis, I'm committed. Do you know the difference between involvement and commitment? Think of ham and eggs. The chicken is involved. The pig is committed.

Martina Navratilova, US tennis player

Experience is a great advantage. The problem is that when you get the experience, you're too damned old to do anything about it.

Jimmy Connors, US tennis player

...and the Other Sports

The fascination of shooting as
a sport depends almost wholly
on whether you are at the right
or wrong end of the gun.

P. G. Wodehouse

The only athletic sport I ever
mastered was backgammon.

Douglas Jerrold, playwright (1803–1857)

The Oxford rowing crew
– eight minds with but a
single thought, if that.

Max Beerbohm

Jogging is for people who
aren't intelligent enough
to watch television.

Victoria Wood, British comedienne

———•———

I once jogged to the ashtray.

Will Self, British novelist, reviewer and columnist,
when asked by *The Idler* if he had ever had
any encounters with sport and exercise

———•———

The first time I see a jogger
smiling, I'll consider it.

Joan Rivers, US actress, commenting
on when she will start jogging

We used to say
that frisbee is
really a religion –
'Frisbeeterians,' we'd
call ourselves. When
we die, we don't go
to purgatory, we
just land up on the
roof and lie there.

Ed Headrick, inventor of the frisbee (1924–2002)

Bridge is the only game that bruises more shins than hockey.

Unknown

Of course I have played outdoor games. I once played dominoes in an open air café in Paris.

Oscar Wilde

The problem with winter sports is that – follow me closely here – they generally take place in winter.

Unknown

I think my favourite sport in the Olympics is the one where you make your way through the snow, you stop, you shoot a gun, and then continue on. In most of the world it is known as the biathlon, except in New York City, where it is known as winter.

Michael Ventre, US sportswriter

Crystallising my feelings about the game, I find that squash is less frustrating than golf, less fickle than tennis. It is easier than badminton, cheaper than polo. It is better exercise than bowls, quicker than cricket, less boring than jogging, drier than swimming, safer than hang gliding.

John Hopkins, *Squash: A Joyful Game*

The word 'aerobics' came about when the gym instructors got together and said: If we're going to charge $10 an hour, we can't call it 'jumping up and down'.

Rita Rudner, US comedienne

I never did like
working out – it
bears the same
relationship to real
sport as masturbation
does to real sex.

David Lodge, British critic and novelist

At Harvard, he was a very avid
and skilful poker player. One
of the secrets of a successful
poker player is to encourage your
opponent to bet a lot of chips on
a losing hand. This is a pattern of
behaviour one sees repeatedly in
George W. Bush's political career.

**Thomas Lifson, contemporary of
President Bush at university**

———

These trainers aren't for
show – I am an athlete.

Andy Fordham, 30-stone BDO world darts champion

Wrestling is ballet with violence.

Jesse Ventura, American governor of Minnesota

———

I learned long ago, never to
wrestle with a pig; you get dirty,
and besides, the pig likes it.

George Bernard Shaw

Karate is a form
of martial arts in
which people who
have had years and
years of training
can, using only their
hands and feet,
make some of the
worst movies in the
history of the world.

Unknown

I say, let's banish bridge. Let's find some pleasant way of being miserable together.

Don Herald, US humorist (1889–1966)

I was watching sumo wrestling on the television for two hours before I realised it was darts.

Hattie Hayridge, British comedienne

This is a sport where you can talk about sequins, earrings and plunging necklines – and you are talking about the men.

Christine Brennan, US journalist, on ice skating

Biography, like big game
hunting, is one of the recognised
forms of sport, and it is [as]
unfair as only sport can be.

Philip Guedalla, British historian
and writer (1889–1944)

The only weights I lift are my dogs.

Olivia Newton-John, Australian singer and actress

Today I'll discuss a sport that is more relaxing as well as far more fragrant: Dog-sled-riding.'

Dave Barry

———•———

I figure the faster I pedal, the faster I can retire.

Lance Armstrong, cyclist

It's a good idea to begin at
the bottom in everything
except in learning to swim.

Unknown

Playing polo is like trying to play
golf during an earthquake.

Sylvester Stallone

Winning and Losing

We didn't lose the game;
we just ran out of time.

Vince Lombardi, American football coach (1913–1970)

If at first you don't succeed,
you're running about average.

M. H. Alderson

Victory goes to the player who
makes the next-to-last mistake.

Savielly Grigorievitch Tartakower,
chess player (1887–1956)

Winning is not a sometime thing; it's an all time thing. You don't win once in a while, you don't do things right once in a while, you do them right all the time. Winning is a habit. Unfortunately so is losing.

Vince Lombardi

———

The finish line is sometimes merely the symbol of victory. All sorts of personal triumphs take place before that point, and the outcome of the race may actually be decided long before the end.

Laurence Malone, US cycle champion

———

Why they call a feller that keeps losin' all the time a good sport gits me.

Kin Hubbard, US humorist and writer (1868–1930)

Serious sport has nothing to do with fair play. It is bound up with hatred, jealousy, boastfulness, disregard of all rules and sadistic pleasure in witnessing violence. In other words, it is war minus the shooting.

George Orwell, British author (1903–1950)

The minute you start talking
about what you're going to do
if you lose, you have lost.

George Shultz, US racing driver

If I lose at play, I blaspheme; if
my fellow loses, he blasphemes.
So, God is always the loser.

John Donne, British poet (1572–1631)

Finish last in your league
and they call you an idiot.
Finish last in medical school
and they call you Doctor.

Abe Lemons, basketball coach (1923–2002)

Children in British schools are taught to lose gracefully, often at the expense of winning. The real encounter is won in the changing room after the event, in which the extraordinary grace of the loser makes the victory seem hollow and even vaguely indecent to the winner.

Peter Ustinov, *Dear Me*

There are one hundred and ninety-nine ways to get beat, but only one way to win; get there first.

Willie Shoemaker, US jockey (1931–2003)

The difference between try and triumph is just a little umph!

Marvin Phillips, Trinidad goalkeeper

We can't win at home
and we can't win on
the road. My problem
as general manager
is I can't think of
another place to play.

Pat Williams, basketball and baseball executive

Winning is everything. The only ones who remember you when you come second are your wife and your dog.

Damon Hill, British racing driver

However beautiful the strategy, you should occasionally look at the results.

Winston Churchill

If a tie is like kissing your sister, losing is like kissing your grandmother with her teeth out.

George Brett, US baseball player

Extra Time

He did a much better job than I did. He looked like a starfish with jelly legs to me but it worked.

Liverpool's 'spaghetti legs' goalkeeper Bruce Grobbelaar pays tribute to Jerzy Dudek

───────

It's always great fun getting attacked. One of the highlights of my career. He got fined £100 for that but they had a whip-round in the pub and he got £200.

Manager Gordon Strachan on being attacked by a Celtic fan while playing for Aberdeen in 1980

───────

You should only say good things when somebody leaves. Robert has gone – good!

Newcastle chairman Freddy Shepherd over the departure of player Laurent Robert to Portsmouth

Birmingham City, the only team never to have scored during a reign of the Pope.

Jasper Carrott, after the death of Pope John Paul I

If I could win Wimbledon 10 times I'd be happy.

Maria Sharapova, tennis player

I'm very jealous – one of his biceps is bigger than my chest.

BBC tennis commentator John Lloyd on French Open champion Rafael Nadal

---

I really got into watching Becker when I was four or five. I was in my living room and he was in his living room – on centre court.

Roger Federer, tennis player, on his hero Boris Becker

I've got the drinkers and the smokers and the eaters on my side. They like what we do.

John Daly, golfer

It's the best thing to happen to a sport, that you have a superstar. In football there is always something to write about the Beckhams, same as people want to write about Rooney or Hooney or whatever his bloody name is.

Formula One boss Bernie Ecclestone

Also Available

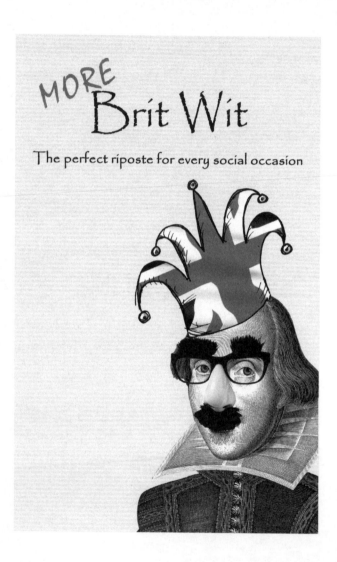

MORE
Brit Wit

The perfect riposte for every social occasion

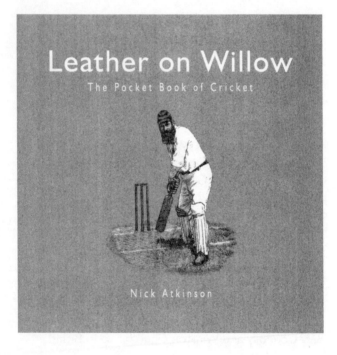

Leather on Willow
The Pocket Book of Cricket

Nick Atkinson

Leather on Willow

The Pocket Book of Cricket

Nick Atkinson

£4.99 Hb

Are you stumped by cricket and would like to know more? Whether you want to test your expert knowledge of the gentleman's game or have simply run out of gift ideas, this is the book for you. Prepare to be bowled over and caught out by this fantastic selection of quotes, anecdotes, jokes and hints on the enduring spectacle that is the game of cricket.

www.summersdale.com